TRUST
HIM

WALKING IN THE
ANOINTED POWER OF GOD
THROUGH TRUST!

Order this book online at www.trafford.com
or email orders@trafford.com

Most Trafford titles are also available at major online book retailers.

Cover design by Reelproductions, Inc., Charlotte, NC.,
www.webmaster@reelproductions.org

Print information available on the last page.

ISBN: 978-1-4120-1164-8 (sc)

Trafford rev. 06/05/2019

Trafford PUBLISHING® www.trafford.com

North America & international
toll-free: 1 888 232 4444 (USA & Canada)
fax: 812 355 4082

REFERENCES

✳

BY

VERA CARROLL

IN LOVING MEMORY OF
MY MOM
VIVIAN T. WARREN

April 26, 1920 —— December 2, 2003

ACKNOWLEDGMENTS

Thanks to the following people for the encouragement given to me to write this book. Even when I doubted and tried to put it aside, one—if not all of you—were there to push me forward to give God the glory.

Susan Wood
Carolyn Wilson
Michelle Gladney-Kelley
Minister Gloria Garner
Pastor Daryle Garner
Pastor Gwathney Leak

A special thanks to Susan Wood, a long time friend from my days in Greensboro, NC, who took the time to take my many notes of encouragement that was sent to a list of my e-mail friends, and returned them to me in the form of a book, encouraging me to publish my writings, that will soon be published in my next book, "Pearls of Wisdom," and the magazine "Woman2Woman".

(www.womantowoman.com)

Thanks to my Pastor, Rev. Daryle Garner, and his wife and my friend, Gloria, for their support all along the way. Your words often shocked me back into reality and encouraged me to move on.

Thanks to Pastor Gwathney Leak, Sr. for planting the seed of encouragement in me to publish my writings long before I could even think it possible.

May God bless each of you as you travel the road of victory in Christ Jesus.

✳

CONTENTS

Introduction
"The Struggle"

Throughout life we have so many obstacles that prevent us from living that trusting faith walk with God. These obstacles render us unfruitful and powerless and prevent us from having that intimate relationship with Him. It is my desire that every child of God will open up their minds to freely receive as God freely gives.

At times in my life I've found myself asking God, "Where is the power? Where is the authority over Satan?" when I found myself going through many trials and tribulations. Over a period of time, God simply walked me through my troubled life and began to show me the depths of His Word. As my life evolved as a Christian I struggled with turning loose and letting God take care of me. Letting God have the problem was easy enough to say, but did I really let go? Was I really able to trust Him?

I think that many of us struggle with the same issue of faith and trust in God, and what He says He will do in His word. We believe His Word is true, but do we really believe He will do it for us? We are connecting to the Word, yet we are very distracted by life's events. The distractions overwhelm us because they are real. They grip our hearts, our minds, and often feel as if they will destroy our very soul. The doctor says you're dying and the pain in your body is intense. You feel and see all the symptoms of the sickness. It's staring you right in the face. That's not hard to believe because your flesh can recognize, relate too, and validate that this is happening. You have heard and read about others who have had similar problems, and you saw the end results they experienced. So you have all the natural proof needed for your mind and heart to have faith in what the doctor says. In the natural it is real and happening to you. All the signs are there and you don't have to wonder, hope, or guess.

Then there is what the Word says about your situation and how God sees you. He says, "by His (Jesus') stripes you are healed." He says "Trust in the Lord, and He will direct your path," and "many are the afflictions of the righteous, but the Lord will deliver you from them all." There are hundreds of other scriptures that could be used to express what God says about your situation and why He is asking you to trust Him. It may be all you have: these words that are on the pages of the Bible, or that come to you from the pulpit, from a friend or at Bible study; these are words that you have been told are filled with power and authority over Satan. The Word of God says to write them upon your heart, and keep your heart and mind stayed on Him.

Under pressure of trials and tribulations, these words can seem so far away. They leave no question of what God desires to do and will do: Yet why do you feel troubled, worried, distressed and fearful? You have read, recited, and heard these scriptures many times. You may have shared or taught them to someone else, expressing the power and authority given to God's children. However, there is that time when there is a shadow of doubt or that question of, "Will He do it for me?" This is the attitude, to my regret, of many Christians today. We face our trials with double-mindedness, fear, and yes, even doubt. We resolve problems that we are faced with not by spiritual intervention, but through worldly resolution. This type of resolution often creates future problems. We find ourselves in a revolving door; going around in circles, never really knowing the victory that is ours as joint heirs with Christ Jesus.

My first experience with seeing someone trust in God was with my oldest brother, Harvey, and his wife, Clastinia. They accepted Christ as their personal savior long before I wanted to even think about it. I saw them pick up and move to Texas to attend Bay Ridge Christian College- because God said so. Even though my family had been raised in church, we all thought this was strange behavior. You don't just have a job and a family that consisted of two small children, sell everything, and just move to Texas. Yet they did, and God blessed them many times, with many stories of miracles and answered prayer.

The old car they drove to Texas came from a junk yard. My brother's father-in-law did some repairs to the car and said a prayer that they would make it to their destination. With many stares along the highway, they arrived safely. For a period of time, that same car served as a campus taxi-cab for many foreign students who did not have transportation. They would voluntarily drive the students or give them the keys to the car to run errands. Once out of school, that same car, brings them back to Greensboro, NC safely.

Then there was the time my family went on vacation, back in the late seventies, with them in a station wagon that could be called anything but reliable for the trip we were about to take. We were headed to Detroit, Canada, Chicago and Anderson, Indiana. I was the skeptic, but they were so relentless in wanting us to go with them, that I didn't know how to say "no," without explaining I didn't have the faith for it. One thing that stayed in my mind was how they always prayed before starting out each day. They depended totally on God for their safety.

While headed back to North Carolina from Anderson, Indiana, which was our last stop on this trip, we were on the stretch of highway from Indiana into Kentucky. We were driving happily down the highway, when my brother mentioned a noise coming from the front wheel of the car. It wasn't constant, so we initially didn't pay much attention to it.

After continuing several miles, we approached an exit when my brother instructed my husband to take the exit immediately, and with a sense of urgency. He explained, "God says to get off here." So we did with a bit of confusion. "Why does it have to be this exit?" I thought.

We found a service station where they asked him to check the wheels. The man came out after about five or ten minutes with a look of shock. He began explaining that the wheel was almost off and was shocked that it had remained on in the condition it was in. I haven't a clue what was broken, but it was enough for me to understand that no wheel at 60 MPH was not good. The serviceman said he would have the part by early morning, and we could be on our way by 10:00 AM. So we praised God, because He had kept us safe and brought us to an exit with a service station, and a hotel right next door.

The next morning we were back on the highway just as the man had stated, but we found there was more to why we needed to get off the highway at that exit. Not more than four or five miles down the road, we entered the mountains with cliffs off the highway. We all became speechless, as we realized why God's instructions were to get off at that particular exit. It was the last exit before we were to enter an extremely dangerous area. If the tire had come off, there was nowhere to go but down or plow into oncoming traffic and the side of a mountain. There were no service stations or gas stations for the next ten to fifteen miles-just mountains. Eventually, we rejoiced once we got over the shock. God was an on-time God.

It was these types of events and miracles that got my attention. Their lives have been filled with many more stories that the only answer that can be given is: "God." It was during those days that my life changed, as I began to realize God is on the throne and waiting for us to trust Him. Developing that trust has taken me years of struggle, as I have had opportunity to experience many disappointments and trials, but as I learn to trust, God brings me through.

What my desire with the words in this book is to move you forward to a life of trust, faith and victory as we are faced with countless attacks from the enemy. We must realize that God has not forgotten us or left us to go it alone. He is there in the midst of the storm.

✳

I

Follow the Recipe

Many years ago, I was making what my mother called, "Sweet Breakfast Pickles." The process of making these delicious pickles takes a number of days. If I remember correctly, it takes about a week. The pickles have to sit in lime for a few days, and then sugar and vinegar for a few more days.

If you don't follow the recipe, you don't get the pickles that taste like none other. I'm here to tell you that they just will not be the same. Without the lime, they will not be crisp. Without the correct amount of sugar, they will not have the exact sweetness that makes them so delicious. So it is with any other recipe. Any other variation and it won't be the same as anticipated.

If grandma gives you her recipe for molasses cake, then it's necessary to do all the things that grandma has listed in order to come up with the same taste and flavor. It's necessary to follow the recipe if we want the same results.

As a Christian, if we want the end results to be what God intended and obtain the results that are ours by inheritance as joint heirs with Christ Jesus, then we need to follow the recipe that has been provided for us. That recipe book is the Word of God, the Bible. The Bible has instructions for anything we can encounter in life. If you want to make peace with someone, the instructions are in the book. If you want to know how to love, it's in the book. If you want to know how to walk in faith, it's in the book. Every situation is covered. The real challenge is getting to a point in your walk with God that you really trust in God enough to believe all that His Word says and then walk in obedience.

The trouble that we first encounter is that we start out with intentions of walking by faith, loving everyone as ourselves, and pleasing God, but we don't follow the instructions in our guide to get results. We end up doing it our way.

What we get is a cake that looks like a cake until we cut it open. It falls, or could be too dry. It's heavy in the center and just doesn't taste or look good. We try to cover it up with some delicious tasty icing; but once you get past that, it's just not what it appears to be. Nobody wants it, nor do they want anything like it. It ends up being good for nothing. You're destined for failure as a child of God if you don't follow the instructions in the Book.

The Bible tells us we are the salt of the earth. We have to set the example for others to follow. However, what we experience is people don't even want to taste what we have. They can tell it's only sugar-coated or simply covered with icing. The end result is that we are ineffective and bear no fruit. We are ineffective in our prayer life, and our total Christian walk. No signs are following, and once others have tasted of what we say we have, they don't want any more. What is needed is a total surrender to God and a life filled with prayer to get us on the faith path that God desires.

James 5:16 tells us that 'the effectual fervent prayers of a righteous man availeth much.'

This means a Christian who knows how to pray in faith can get results.

Elijah prayed for rain, and it rained. He then prayed that it would stop and it stopped. He was obviously following the recipe. He trusted that God would do what He said He would do.

Moses was a man with a vision. The Lord told him that He would use him to set the Israelites free and take them to the promise land. He followed the Instructions time after time after time to get the end results. The vision was made alive. The Israelites were set free. Even as they were in the desert, he followed God's instructions. Then Moses decided, after seeing so many times that following God's instructions (His recipe) worked, to disobey and the results cost Him the opportunity to enter into the Promised Land. We take chances and basically we are depending on luck, which is not God's desire.

❊

Yes, yes I see it now, I see the answer. You might get it: Oh wait.... Maybe not..... I am sorry! It appears you don't follow instructions: therefore, your great blessing has vanished before my eyes.

❊

As Christians, we obviously don't want to entrust our future to the stars, but with the way we disobey God, we are taking that type of chance daily. Our blessings only become things we dream about. We miss our promised land. We are missing victories because we won't follow the recipe. Many of us won't even open The Book to see what it's telling us to do, and when we do, we alter the instructions.

It's like your mom telling you to put in a dozen eggs, and you decide that you'll only use six eggs, but yet you expect the same results. We make lasagna, and leave out the cheese, but we expect it to taste like lasagna. Then we complain about how we tried to fix lasagna and it didn't work. Well what did you expect?

Oh, yea, I forgot, a miracle. We always expect God to just drop right in, fix our problems, give us the victory, give us the best life we can dream up, but we won't follow the instructions to get those kind of results that belong to us as believers.

If I asked you if you were selfish, you would probably answer, "No". But unless you have resolved to follow God's instruction book, you probably have very selfish prayer requests of God. Fix this, God fix that—even down to— make me a better Christian, Lord, more faithful, loving, and kind. We will even tell Him we want the anointing to operate in our lives, when all we really need to do is follow the instruction book. If we will follow the Bible's instructions, a Spirit-filled Christian-with signs following-will evolve, operating with more love, kindness, faith, and trust.

My prayer for you is that you will resolve in your heart to do The Word; not just hear it and continue on as you are today. If you find yourself short on following the recipes given in The Word of God, then start today allowing God to deliver you from all the things that so easily beset you and allowing Him to free you from bondage of your sinful nature. "Resist the devil and he will flee." **(James 4:7)** Resist the temptation to continue as you are. To resist requires action. It requires you to defy or stand firm.

One night, I found myself watching one of the many TV programs where some person is trying to avoid being arrested by a police officer whose first intent was to stop the person and simply write them a ticket. What appeared to be a simple traffic violation turns into a high speed chase with the individual traveling down the highway at a high rate of speed. The police toss out the spikes in front of the out-of-control car to flatten the tires, but the individual continues on what eventually become tireless rims. Sparks are flying from beneath the car as it continues down the highway out of control with the individual continuing to resist being arrested. Once the car cannot go any further on its rims, they stop the car, and begin to run.

The police officer eventually catches the individual after an intense foot pursuit where they have to wrestle them to the ground. It usually takes two or three police officers to get them into the handcuffs, and the individual is still fighting with all their might. They are willing to experience some pain to gain their freedom and avoid the penalty of their actions.

As I watched, God spoke to my spirit, "This is how you resist." When you resist the devil, you've got do more than just say it. Resisting will require you to fight to gain your freedom from whatever has you bound. The fight will cause pain to your flesh, because the flesh will not get what it desires if you are resisting.

Resisting is more than trying not to do a thing. You need to be determined not to give in regardless of how much your flesh suffers. You fight to do what the Spirit desires, rather than giving in to your flesh. It may cause tears to flow. It may cause repentance. It may cause you to stay in prayer all night-but to resist is necessary to create the change that will move you to an intimate and close relationship with God.

To resist the devil is following the recipe that God has provided in His Word. To resist means you defy and stand against the thing that has you bound, to gain your freedom In Christ Jesus.

The result of staying with the recipe means change in you, and when there is a change in you that follows the path God has set, you gain the victory. This type of change means the power of the Holy Spirit working in your life. It means that you will come forth as pure gold through every trial and every hard time because God will bring you out. Following the instructions means you can trust in God to honor every promise in His Word. Remember Samuel's words to Saul that obedience is better than sacrifice *(I Samuel 15:22)* To follow the instructions in God's Word is obedience to Him.

If you are living a defeated life as a Christian, make sure you are adding all the ingredients to get the results in God's promises. The oven is already hot. The anointing is waiting on you to trust and obey, for there is no other way. The commitment to do all of God's commandments positions us to walk in His anointed power.

I often wonder if we think God has gone to sleep and is not noticing how disobedient we are. We have made excuses for our disobedience, but we expect to get the promises. Keep your prayer line open by being obedient to God. If disobedience is breaking the connection, don't expect to receive anything but God's mercy. Through His loving mercy, God may grant your desires, but don't confuse that with the blessings of your inheritance as a joint heir with Christ Jesus. God says He rains on the just as well as the unjust.

It is so easy to fall into the trap set by the evil one, that it's acceptable to live disobedient to God. He wants us to stay confused because He doesn't want you to connect to the power of God and live victorious as an overcomer. Do not be deceived. God desires us to obey. If you want to be blessed by God, then live obedient and follow the recipe.

✳

2

Worry—A Lack of Trust

To fret, fear, be concerned, lose sleep, or be bothered. Be anxious, troubled, or agonize over.

"For God hath not given us the spirit of fear, but of power, and of love, and of a sound mind." II Timothy 1:7

I think everyone would agree, worrying doesn't help any situation, but often creates other problems in the life of the one that is worrying. Worry we all know causes stress, and stress can cause frustration, fear, anger, and anxiety; which can all lead to sickness. I have heard that eventually stress may cause your immune system to stop protecting itself from the various diseases that may attack the human body.

This is one method in which Satan uses to kill, steal, and destroy. He loves to flood our lives with fear, doubt, and discouragement. It is the tool he uses to prevent us from walking in victory and ultimately creating a double-minded

Christian that isn't walking by faith—therefore not truly trusting nor obeying God.

I can't say that worry doesn't change anything in our lives; because it may change when we will see the thing we have asked God for; causing the outcome to be less than what God desires for us. This also creates a less than desirable situation for us by prolonging the trial and never really receiving the victory that is ours by being joint heirs with Jesus Christ.

Worry is what many Christians experience while going through trials and tribulations we are faced with day to day. Satan desires to destroy your trust in God, which directly affects the quality of your Christian walk.

If he can steal the Word of God from you, then he can make you doubt, and that is his intent. What we must realize is that when worry comes in, the Word is going out.

Where there is worry, fear exists. Where there is fear, there is no power over the enemy. If there is no power over the enemy, then we find ourselves with out trust in God, which directly affects our love walk and faith in God.

Worry creates a double mind and not the sound mind that God desires us to have. No matter how hard we try to trust that things will work out to the glory of God, doubt arises and chokes out the Word, giving no benefit and producing the opposite of God's Word.

It is in the middle of the worrying that we come up with our own ideas about what to do, what to say, how to act, etc. **Our own methods of resolution just get in God's way.** It's the "give it to God, but then take it back" that is keeping us from the victory we have a right to as over-comers in the household of God.

> *(I John 5:1-5)* "*Everyone who believes that Jesus is the Christ is born of God; and everyone who loves the Father loves His child as well. This is how we know that we love the children of God: by loving God and carrying out his commands. This is love for God: to obey his commands. and his commands are not burdensome, for everyone born of God overcomes the world. This is the*

victory that has overcome the world, even our faith. Who is it that overcomes the world? Only he who believes that Jesus is the Son of God."

These words written by the apostle John, clearly tell us that when we become Christians, we become members of God's family. It was never promised that we wouldn't have problems, but He did promise that He would help us to bear each burden and that he who believes in Jesus Christ overcomes the world. This tells me that in the end, we will win!

This passage of scripture also says that we must carry out the commandments of God to be overcomers, which represents your love for Him. *Obedience is better than sacrifice.* So we must obey his commands. We must follow the recipe, and trust that God will do exactly what He says He will do.

This next scripture should set our expectations as Christians. *Psalm 34:19* says, *"A righteous man may have many troubles, but the Lord delivers him from them all."* It clearly states that we shall have many problems but we have a promise of deliverance. We desire that problems become nonexistent in our life, but that's not going to happen. It may be sickness, grief, failures, family problems, or the frustration of our daily existence. Regardless, God promises to be there. He promises to deliver us out of every situation. Sometimes the trouble you are experiencing may be what God will use to develop your strength and wisdom as He guides you through, for the Lord has never forsaken those that seek him *(Psalm 9:10)*. David also said it like this in *Psalm 37:25, "I was young and now I am old, yet I have never seen the righteous forsaken, or their children begging bread."*

Though you have many troubles, God is always there, just as he was with Joseph when his brothers sold him to slavery. Just as he was with Moses when he faced the many troubles of his life before he was able to take his place and lead the Israelites out of Egypt. Just as he was with Paul in prison as he writes the book of Philippians and talks about having joy, and peace. David found himself running and hiding from King Saul but he as able to write the *23rd Psalm, "The Lord is my Shepherd; I shall not want."* The truth of the matter is, God has not left you nor will He leave you in the midst of your troubles. The command is for you to follow after Him, to know His desires and His ways, and He will see you through. Not your way—but God's way—of going through. Realize that God may not cause the problem, but He sure knows how to end it.

Many of us, when faced with a problem, will use the world's way to resolve the problem. We see seconds turn to minutes, minutes turn to hours, hours turn to days, and days to months. Yes, often years go by and we don't have the thing we have been praying for. The problem still exists, so we live, miserably, in disbelief.

The bills are due so we worry until we can figure out from whom to borrow the money. If we had held out and trusted God, He would have provided a means that would not require us to borrow money from anyone. It's when the car needs repair that we worry and ponder over it until we resolve that we need to get into debt and purchase a new one, which could very easily result in a new problem.

Then there's the teenager that just will not act right; so we pray, and worry, and talk with our friends about it—until they tell you what they did to fix their problem. We try the friend's suggestion and when that fails we say, "God what now?" "I've tried everything and the situation continues to get worse despite all my efforts. Why won't you help me?"

We even worry and stress out over our relationship with God and wonder why God won't answer our prayers. Our prayer may not be answered because what we haven't really tried is to wait on the Lord and trust that He will show you a way out, or show you what to do. Some time in my past, I recall hearing it described this way, *"To worry is to doubt. To doubt is to sin."* It's direct disobedience of God's Word, as He tells us many times in His Word to trust Him and believe.

God wants us to trust Him and believe that He will do everything He has promised in His Word. The problem lies in our lack of ability to trust that He will come through for us. We say the words, *"God is not a man that He would lie, (Numbers 23:19)* or *"For nothing is impossible with God. (Luke 1:37),* but do we believe what we say? Our actions of worry and questioning of God about what He is doing and why, indicate the opposite.

When we come to the realization that God's promises can't be broken, we also must realize that with every promise comes a requirement that we must be obedient in all that He says in His Word and to anything that He has asked us to do. This includes trusting Him regardless of how bad your situation may appear and to have faith in Him and in His Word, for *'it is impossible to please God without faith" (Hebrews 11:6)*.

It is time for God's children to realize that *"God did not give us a spirit of fear, but of power, love and a sound mind," II Timothy 1:7.* When fear, frustration, worry and anxiety appear in our lives, we must quickly realize who is responsible and begin to walk in the power that God has given us as His children. If we continue to worry, we continue to serve the one that actually causes our problems, and that, my friend, is sin. It is time for us to remember, *"No weapon formed against us will prosper" Isaiah 54:17.* The weapon may form, but God will bring you out of every situation.

With this type of support, why worry? The answer and resolution is with one that is much greater than I. He sees all my problems; He's working daily to bring them to an end. It is I who step in and cause the delay. It is I who fail to trust Him.

✳

3

EXPERIENCING FEAR?

Fear: Dread, fright, alarm, apprehension

WHAT DO YOU DO?

The Word of God should be alive in your heart and represent your walk with God. What I mean by alive is that it has taken root in your heart. When someone watches you in your daily activity, regardless of the event, they see the Word of God in action.

The Word is like a seed that is planted and has to take root in order to produce. Once it starts its transition, the possibilities of what could happen or might happen, don't stop it from growing. It is at that point that the seed is what it is going to be unless it is not nourished. The end results of that seed will be based upon it getting enough nourishment to produce. **It is difficult to produce if the Word of God is only in your mind and not written and living in your heart.** To produce anything to the glory of God the Word of God in you has to be nourished daily, so that it takes root in the heart. If it is truly in your heart, it is what you will think of regardless of the circumstances that surround you. What is written upon your heart is how you will see yourself. That reminds me of the old saying, "what you see is what you will get", or maybe I should say, it is what you will become.

To overcome the fear of death, sickness, diseases, war, terrorism or any problem we can be faced with we must find scriptures like the following rooted and grounded in our hearts. There are many things that confront us on a daily basis that a few years back was never a thought. Now things have changed and a complete trust in God and His promises is the best way to continue to avoid being overtaken in fear.

For God hath not given us the spirit of fear, but of power, and of love, and of a sound mind. **II Timothy 1:7**

For ye nave not received the spirit of bondage again to fear, but ye have received the Spirit of adoption, whereby we cry, Abba, Father. **Romans**

8:15 There is no fear in love; but perfect love casteth out fear; because fear hath torment. He that feareth is not made perfect in love. **I John 4:18**

He that dwelleth in the secret place of the most High shall abide under the shadow of the Almighty. **Psalm 91:1**

He shall cover thee with his feathers, and under his wings shalt thou trust: his trust shall be thy shield and buckler. Thou shalt not be afraid for the terror by night; nor for the arrow that flieth by day; Nor for the pestilence that walketh in darkness; nor for the destruction that wasteth at noonday. A thousand shall fall at thy side, and ten thousand at thy right hand; but it shall not come nigh thee. **Psalm 91:4-7**

There shall no evil befall thee, neither shall any plague come nigh thy dwelling, For he shall give his angels charge over three, to keep thee in all thy ways. **Psalms 91:10,11**

Be not afraid of sudden fear, neither of the desolation of the wicked, when it cometh. For the Lord shall be thy confidence, and shall keep thy foot from being taken. **Proverbs 3:25,26**

In righteousness shalt thou be established: thou shalt be far from oppression; for thou shalt not fear: and from terror; for it shall not come near thee. Isaiah 54:14

In God have I put my trust: I will not be afraid what man can do unto me. Psalm 56:11

Yea, thou I walk through the valley of the shadow of death, I will fear no evil; for thou art with me: thy rod and thy staff shall comfort me. Thou preparest a table before me in the presence of mine enemies: thou anointest my head with oil; my cup runneth over. Psalm 23:4, 5

For whom he did foreknow, he also did predestinate to be conformed to the image of his Son, that he might be the firstborn among many brethren. What shall we then say to these things? If God be for us, who can be against us? Who shall separate us from the love of Christ? Shall tribulation, or distress, or persecution, or famine, or nakedness, or peril, or sword? As it is written, For thy sake we are killed all the day long; we are accounted as sheep for the slaughter. Nay, in all these things we are more than conquerors through him that loved us. For I am persuaded, that neither death, nor life, nor angels, nor principalities, nor powers, nor things present, nor things to come, nor height, nor depth, nor any other creature, shall be able to separate us from the love of God, which is in Christ Jesus our Lord. **Romans 8:29, 31-39**

Be of good courage, and he shall strengthen your heart, all ye that hope in the Lord. **Psalms 31:24**

Peace I leave with you, my peace I give unto you: not as the world giveth, give I unto you. Let not. your heart be troubled, neither let it be afraid". **John 14:27**

The Lord is my light and my salvation; whom shall I fear? The Lord is the strength of my life: of who shall I be afraid? Though an host should encamp against me, my heart shall not fear; though war should rise against me, in this will I be confident. **Psalms 27:1-3**

So that we may boldly say, The Lord is my helper, and I will not fear what man shall do unto me. **Hebrews 13:6**

I am completely and totally persuaded that we should not live in fear. For *"God did not give us a spirit of fear, but of power, and love and a sound mind" (II Timothy 1:7).* This tells me we should walk in faith that no harm shall come to us, and that God is our protector and provider for whatever the situation is. The spirit of fear has to come from the evil one, Satan. **To fear is lack of trust in God and in His promises to you.** Fear may come when you are faced with problems, such as how to pay the mortgage, when there's no money in the bank, the child is in a car accident and is being rushed to the hospital, or you get a bad report from the doctor. There are various things that may grip us with fear, but the reality based upon the Word of God is that He didn't give us a spirit of fear. Satan desires to frighten us, with hopes that we will be gripped with fear. It's his strategy to keep us from our victory. Continuing in fear brings us to a lack of faith and trust in God to bring us out of whatever we are facing.

It is not the initial reaction in my opinion that removes us from our faith walk, but it is continued fear, which says to God: "I don't trust you to care for me". The natural reaction may be to fear, but the spiritual reaction—once the initial shock is over—is to stand in faith and trust God. The problem that many of us have with being able to stand in faith—after the initial shock of a situation—is that fear has a greater hold in our hearts than our belief in

God's promises. We have not allowed the Word to become written upon our hearts. So when the fear comes, there is no word to fight in the battle. No Word to fight, then fear wins the battle and we are overcome.

The Word tells us that *"No weapon formed against us shall prosper" (Isaiah 54:17)*. That means sickness, poverty, your enemies, problems, etc. The real fact is no weapon means not even one can overtake you.

I suggest that we commit these scriptures of trust and confidence of the Lord in our lives to memory. Plant them in your heart, which will build your faith. How else can we fight the darts of the evil one when he comes to make us afraid or doubt, except to be able to remember what God is saying to us and about us. *Ephesians 6:16* says, *"Above all, taking the shield of faith, wherewith ye shall be able to quench all the fiery darts of the wicked."* Not some of the darts, but all of the darts. If God's Word has taken root in your heart, it will grow faith, and faith will fight against everything that comes to you from the evil one. Paul gave several instructions in how to be prepared for battle, but he makes it very clear with those two words, "above all". So you can't do spiritual warfare without your primary weapon which is faith.

When we face situations that cause fear, the only thing we can think of is the situation and its possible outcome. Why is this? We have not become consumed with the Word of God. The Word has not become alive to us. It still remains to be words on a page. We need the Word living in us, so that when we think about life and all its situations we should remember and know the scripture that presents God's promise to us. Our confidence should be more in the Word than in what is physically active in our lives. Confidently realizing we are children of the King; therefore we are joint heirs with Jesus *(Romans 8:17, Galatians 4:7)*. A joint heir has the right to everything that has been promised, and that's the attitude Christians should have. An heir trusts that they will receive everything promised to them, so they rest with an expectation of receiving what has been named as rightfully theirs.

While working on my previous job, I traveled a 55-mile-trip one-way to the location where I was assigned. That time became very valuable to my spiritual growth. I used that time to pray each day as I made the journey to and from work. God began to speak to my heart and direct my path. It became such precious time with God.

One morning on my way to work, after having previously purchased an English translated Bible, I found myself having to face fear head-on. I began to question why I had made this purchase, since I already had an English Bible at home. Not really understanding why I felt lead to buy it that day, I decided to keep it at my desk at work. The next day I placed the Bible in a convenient place on my desk along side my King James Version. I felt good about having it there and really gave it no more thought.

The next day as I pulled into the parking lot, I heard the Holy Spirit say, "give the Bible to an individual that worked with me as a team leader." Fear gripped me, as I quickly realized that might be risky since it was against company policy to express religious views and make others feel uncomfortable. Giving the Bible to someone I was close to wouldn't have frightened me, but giving it to someone that I wasn't sure was even a Christian made me stop and give it some serious thought, as fear gripped my heart. The thought that ran through my mind and created fear was: "What if she gets upset and reports me?" But above all that fear, I could still hear God say, "give her the book." After much struggle, I obeyed. I placed The Bible on her desk with a note or maybe I should say a disclaimer, since the fear of getting in trouble became my primary focus. I scribbled the following sentence on a piece of paper: "If this upsets you, let me know. Just return it to me, because I am not trying to do anything to upset you." Where was my trust and faith in God?

Within a few minutes she was standing at my door with tears in her eyes. I immediately began to apologize; thinking I had angered her to tears. She began to speak; thanking me for the Bible. It was her next words that took my breath away. She asked, "How did you know to give me this?" I explained how it all came about. She then explained that in the previous week, she had picked up a King James Version of the Bible and had thrown it aside; stating,

"God if you want me to understand it, you're going to have to give it to me in English because I just can't understand this." I then began to cry too, as I realized that God was in control. There was nothing to fear because He was answering a request, and I just happened to be the vessel in which he used. This individual made it clear to God what she needed to understand the Word. Isn't that just like Him to meet her skeptical yet simple request? I repented of my fear and continued my desire to trust God without doubt.

Don't let Satan destroy you with fear. Don't let him keep you from victory in your life. *"God is not a man that He will lie" (Numbers 23:19)*. He is faithful to His Word. He will do what He has promised. Trust in God with all that is within you and He will lead, guide, direct and bring you out. Trust that comes from your heart can only come when the Word is BIG and fully matured within you. When the Word becomes your life-first and foremost the way you think everyday, hour and minute, you will be matured in his Word. You will *abide in Him, and His Word abide in you, that you will ask what you will and it shall be done unto you, John 15:7*.

Let's get desperate to walk in victory with anointed power which can only be obtained if we do not walk in fear. The opposite of fear is faith. Faith comes by hearing the Word of God. It's great to be able to hear someone else preach the Word to us, but most of all we must know the Word for ourselves, and live it. It is time for us to get busy. There is no time to waste, Satan is beating down our door, and the only way we can put him in his place is with the Word of God living in and through us. We hear Satan knocking and banging at our door constantly. But our hands are tied and our mouths are gagged, which prevents us from running Satan away or defending our rights. It's time to put on our armor and get ready for battle. It's time to untie our hands, by getting in the Word, allowing it to saturate our hearts and melt away the gag that's in our mouths.

Remember *Ephesians 6* refers to the Word of God as your sword. Faith is your shield and the Word is your sword. Don't be comfortable where you are by saying you are walking in faith to battle if you have nothing to destroy the enemy with. You've got your guns, but no ammunition. You've got a fighter jet, but no missiles. The lack of ammunition to fight back always keeps us on the defensive side of the battle. We are able to fly around the enemies heat- seeking missiles, but not able to fight back. This keeps us in constant fear. *Can you visualize that?*

We say we believe, and stand on the Word of God through every battle we go through, but we have no weapon with which to fight back. So the trial goes on, and on, and on, leaving us to wonder why there is no victory in our prayer life.

We stand, continuously in battles thatt last an eternity. We've got our shield up **(Faith that God can do)**, but we have no weapon **(no Word and no trust that God will do what He can do and says He will do for us)**. It's time to load our weapons of warfare. It's time to stop fear dead in its tracks.

Let us stop quoting and singing scriptures from memory with no root of that word in our heart. You will never be able to quench the fiery darts

of the enemy if the Word does not live in your
heart..

＊

4

DISCOURAGED?

Disheartened, depressed, downcast or unenthusiastic.

Let not your heart be troubled: Ye believe in God, believe also in me. John 14:1

In studying this scripture, I quickly realized that discouragement is not what God intended for his children. Many times we find ourselves discouraged with feelings of defeat. Pondering over some misfortune or problem and wondering why, asking questions like: What did I do wrong? When will it end? We allow our emotions to take us to a place that is neither enjoyable, nor sanctioned by God. We find ourselves overtaken with discouragement.

John 14:27 says, *"Peace, I leave with you, my peace I give unto you: not as the world giveth, give I unto you. Let not your heart be troubled; neither let it be afraid."* Do you suppose He truly means for us to experience peace when your heart is so troubled or broken? Should this peace exist when someone has wronged you, taken advantage of you, or someone you love very much fails to return that love? Can there be peace when your child's future has just been altered for the worse by some action, situation or event? Where can we find peace?

When I faced many challenges in my life, I personally can remember getting so wrapped up in my own emotions that if you had asked me the above questions, I would have said, "Peace in this world? "Surely not." My life was filled with statements like, "this really hurts." "This can't be happening to me." "I mean, what will I do, how will I survive?" "How could they have been so inconsiderate?" "Surely God has just forgotten me." "He doesn't care or He's upset with me." "What now?" I am not proud of it, but I have truly had all of these emotions and thoughts, and many more that represented nothing that God desired me to believe.

I experienced many of these emotions when I found myself going through a separation in a marriage of fifteen years. I could not conceive that God expected me to experience peace during what appeared to be my life falling apart. I struggled through my days as I read the Word of God, and constantly tried to convince myself that I trusted and believed that God had my best interest at heart. Eventually, I realized I didn't have a true understanding of what it meant to believe in God. The word "believe", means to *trust in, consider true, and in the Biblical sense, have no doubt in.* If something is true, then it can't be a lie, or untruth. **So if I believed that the Word of God is true, why didn't I believe in, trust in, and have no doubt in the Word of God for my life?**

While going through this life-changing situation, all I did as I repeated scriptures to myself was try to convince myself that the words I was repeating were true. I had no faith in what I was repeating as representation of what God would do, wanted to do, and promised to do for me. It wasn't belief that was standing on, but relentlessly trying to persuade myself that God would do exactly what He said, all while I experienced emotions of discouragement and depression. With a failed marriage, I found out repeating words over in my mind would not produce complete trust in the promises of God; when the thing that was before me was the exact opposite. I found out I had to trust the one that said it to make the connection between my head and my heart.

If I could have trusted in, depended upon, relied upon the fact that God will do what He says and that He will never forsake me or leave me, then in the midst of my troubles I could have experienced great peace. Instead, I was focusing on the things of this world to create peace for me. .If God would fix my marriage, I could have peace, and I could trust Him. Then I could somehow say that God was with me, helping me, and that He would never leave me.

My peace was based upon resolution to problems that existed, and not my trust in God. I had no faith or trust in God or His Word. It was only words I tried to convince myself were true and applied to my life. For *faith is the substance of things hoped for and the evidence of things unseen. (Hebrews 12:1)* I was trying to make faith be confidence in the results rather than what I hoped for and could not see.

This kind of attitude of trust basically says to God, "my way is the right way, so let me convince you of that, and oh by the way, do it now so I can really trust you". It wasn't about God being in control. It wasn't the fact that He knew what was best for me. It was all about "hurry up so I can trust in what I am reading and I don't have to go through this emotional stress. I need life to be normal so I can have peace."

The Apostle Paul, in the book of Philippians, talks of experiencing peace-all while he is in prison. The peace he experienced was not based upon his unpleasant situation, but upon his trust and confidence in God. He had every reason to be discouraged, depressed, and disheartened because he was imprisoned for preaching Jesus Christ. It wasn't for being a thief, or killing someone, but because he shared the Word of God. His faith and trust in God resulted in having a peace that surpassed his understanding. His peace was not a result of God giving the flesh relief and what it desired, but simply knowing that God was on his side regardless to how things turned out. Paul knew He had a Godly purpose on this earth and as long as he was fulfilling God's purpose, he was content and filled with peace.

Today our questions and concerns with our problems seem to never end. Yet the Word of God is very plan about this. In *John 14:27* Jesus tells you not worry about anything. He makes it clear that He is leaving His peace with us. Don't take the concern in your heart, because God gives peace, but *not as the world gives peace.* The peace God gives has nothing to do with what you are going through, or any trial you may have just come out of. God's peace is all based upon your intimate relationship with Him. If you have learned to trust and obey His commandments, then you have established an intimate relationship with the Father. You know Him well enough to know that you can trust Him regardless of what's going on in your life. That confidence alone can bring peace beyond anything you can experience in the natural.

Philippians 4:6-8 tells us to *"be careful for nothing; but in everything by prayer and supplication with thanksgiving let your requests be made unto God. and the peace of God, which passeth all understanding shall keep your hearts and minds through Christ Jesus. Finally, whatever is true, honest, just, pure, lovely, of a good report, if anything has any virtue and has any praise, think about these things."* Think on these things—not the problem, not the concern, not the misfortune, and not what you want. If you will think on what is true, honest, pure, lovely, of a good report, or anything that has any virtue and has any praise, then the peace of God that surpasses all your understanding will keep your heart and mind. This clearly encourages us to think on the things of God rather than what happened to us. Thinking on the situation is Satan's foothold on us to keep us discouraged and downhearted.

What we say has an affect on getting Godly results and having the peace of God. The tongue will begin to speak what's in our hearts *(Matthew 12:34),* which is normally what we think on; s*etting on fire, the course of our future (James 3:2-9).* What we say and think can greatly affect the outcome of our trial. To get Godly results, we must speak and think Godly thoughts. It will affect who we become and surely affect the outcome of our problem. Do you choose victory or failure? How you think and what you say will surely determine what you get.

As a joint heir with Christ Jesus, we must have confidence in what we confess from the Word of God, and live all we know to live from the Word. We must rest in our purpose in the kingdom of God and *rejoice that our names are written in heaven (Luke 10:20)*. In fact, it is then we will be able to rejoice and find true peace. Jesus told the messengers that were rejoicing because of their authority over demons that they should not rejoice because of what they were able to accomplish, but rejoice because their names were written in Heaven. With that in mind, it should be shouting ground for every Christian.

It's not God's will for us to carry our burdens. He wants us to continue the faith walk and trust Him to bring us out. Trusting that He will bring you out as pure gold. Think about and learn His word. Feed your heart from good thoughts from the Word of God, and peace will overtake you. He will bring you out....

✳

5

Faith Without Works is Dead.....

James 2:14-26

There are many thought provoking statements in James, but this particular one always catches my attention when the subject of faith comes up. James asked the question, "What doth it profit you to say you have faith, but you have done nothing to show for it?" Can saying you have faith save you, help someone, minister to someone in need, or even show that you trust God completely and entirely? Many of us say that we trust God; that we have faith in Him. But I ask you to carefully think about that statement.

Do you have faith? Do you trust God? Or is it more that you believe that God exists, and that you are aware that He cares about you, and loves you? Please understand that faith is realized and shown by action. It is what you do if you are down to your last dime. To give your last dime away to the glory of God for the cause of God is faith-trusting that God will provide for your own needs. To stand and tell the truth when it isn't popular or could result in persecution is faith. To praise God in the midst of the storm is faith. You see, faith is an action. It's what you do. In Hebrews chapter 11 we find many stories of the faith walk. Each of the individuals in *Hebrews 11* that we will look at did something more than just talk about having faith or talk about what they believed God could do. They took action on a promise even when it looked impossible or fatal.

Abraham trusted that God would provide the ram in the bush, and spare his son from being the sacrifice. Yet he continued to act on what God told him to do. Abraham's faith walk began long before he got to the place where his son's life would be taken as a sacrifice *(Genesis 22)*. In verse 2 Abraham heard God tell him to *"take now your son, your only son Isaac, whom you love, and go to the land of Mariah, and offer him there as a burnt offering on one of the mountains of which I shall tell you."* This is when the faith walk began for Abraham. At this very moment Abraham had to trust God.

God acknowledged or reminded Abraham that it was his only son that he was to sacrifice.

God was not confused about who this child was. He knew that Isaac was a unique miracle child that was born of a woman beyond her years of child bearing. So there was no confusion about who this child was to Abraham and that this child had a divine purpose. God also acknowledged that He knew that Abraham loved him, but God still gave him instructions to give him as a burnt offering.

Abraham did not question God, or complain. He obediently got up the next morning and began his journey. Now take notice that Abraham got up, saddled his donkey, split the wood for the burnt offering, and then arose and went to the place of which God had told him. Abraham did more than just talk about his trust and faith in God—he took action. Each action was taken while in the natural. Abraham had to be emotionally drained from the very thought of having to destroy his only son's precious life. Abraham did this thing, even if it wasn't what felt good to his flesh.

Then the Bible says on the third day Abraham lifted his eyes and saw the place afar off. Abraham had to follow through with his action of obedience these three days. Then leaving behind the two young men that were with him, Abraham took Isaac and said that they would go up to worship. He is talking about worship to God even in the midst of his sorrows. He had an opportunity to complain, or talk about his worries, but he stayed committed to his mission and said they will worship. His next statement was a statement of faith: *"We will come back to you."* He tells the men with him that they will return. Not I will return—but Isaac as well. Abraham continued with his actions of obedience as he took the wood for the burnt offering and laid it on Isaac, while he took the fire and knife in his hand. He stayed focused on what God had told him to do. He didn't look at how he felt, or what he thought. He stepped out on faith, and trusted in God.

As Isaac questioned Abraham about the sacrifice, Abraham made another statement of faith. "My son, God will provide for himself a Lamb for a burnt offering. Abraham was still confessing and stating words of faith, because he knew that God cannot lie, and that all he had to do is trust God regardless of the problem, and He would come through. Once they reached the destination, Abraham continued with actions of obedience, when he built the altar, placed the wood on it, bound Isaac and laid him on it. He then drew back the knife to kill his son. This is when the Angel of the Lord stopped him and said, *"Do not lay your hand to Isaac, for now I know that you fear God, since you have not withheld your son, your only son; from Me."* It was then that Abraham noticed the ram that was caught in the thicket by its horns, which was to be used for the sacrifice.

Abraham went all the way, until it looked as if there was no way out. God waited until it looked like there was no way out before becoming "the God that will provide." Our actions of obedience and trust have to follow through to the end to see the hand of God move in our behalf. He wants to become our provider, but we stop and get off the mission before we reach the end. When God does something, He wants it to be recognizable — that it was something that only He could do. Instead we stop, do a poor job of fixing it ourselves, and try to give God the credit for what we did.

Other acts of faith were shown by Shadrach, Meshach, and Abednego who were willing to take the risk of dying in a furnace if they continued to worship God and prayed to Him when it wasn't the popular thing to do. They went all the way. Rahab, *(James 2:25)* acted in faith by receiving the messengers and saving their lives by sending them another way to protect them. This could have caused her great persecution or death, but she took the risk. She trusted that God would take care of her.

Jesus acted in faith by the things He did. He knew that the Pharisees would not like the things He said and did, but he continued anyway. He knew that His Father in Heaven would care for Him. He didn't wait until a popular time to speak God's word, or clean out the temple of the money changers. He laid hands on the sick when He was moved by compassion and saw their needs. He acted. He didn't wait until he knew it would be safe or when it wouldn't draw criticism... He did His Father's will. He therefore, walked in faith in His Father's plan. He trusted that God, His Father, was on his side.

True faith brings Godly results and is based upon waiting on God to provide rather than seeking man's way to resolve a matter. Abraham set out to use his son as the sacrifice, following God's instructions, not knowing how God was going to work it out. By trusting God, he got divine results. Abraham was also told to go to"' a place that he would receive as his inheritance *(Hebrews 11:8)*. Even though God did not tell Abraham where he was going, he obeyed and *went.* This faith is more than being an usher or singing in the choir. It believes God for the impossible and sees divine results produced. When I think of a Christian in action, my thoughts go to the book of Acts. It was the actions of the Apostles that brought many to Christ. Their works of faith produced results. They could show you their faith through their works. They stood in faith, even when they would suffer persecution. These acts of faith showed they trusted and loved God. **Their faith in God was visible.** There wasn't any question about who they trusted.

We sometimes spend a lot of time waiting on God to move, or give us a word, before we take action, If God says, "Go", then we need to go. We don't need to know why, how, and when before we can begin to act on what He says. Questioning God is an example of dead faith. We say we believe but we don't do anything. We don't witness; we don't share our blessings from God with those in need; we don't minister to others-yet we wait, and wait, and wait.... **Faith without works is dead.** That's what the Word of God says. We pray, and pray and pray for others that we know have needs, but when was the last time we tried to meet that need? We hear of someone who is sick and we go in our closets to pray for them, when what we read in the Word of God is how they laid hands on the sick and prayed for them. They acted and God moved.

The Word says *we shall lay hands on the sick, and they shall recover (Matthew 16:18)*. We stand in our churches waiting for our Pastors to pray for the sick, or we call our Pastors when we hear of someone that is sick so they can pray for them. We run to the next convention or conference to hear from God and that's all great. But when will we act? We continue to hear of a need, and we call the church to see if the church can help with the need-knowing that we have an extra $100.00 left after paying bills that we want to buy a new pair of shoes, which we don't even need.

Once again I say, "many believe that God exists, just as Satan believes in Him and even knows to fear Him. What we must realize is that believing that God exists, is not enough. To truly believe in God is to trust in, depend upon, rely on and have confidence in Him. If we trust in and rely on God, then we must begin to take the faith walk. We must start to act on our faith.

Trusting in Him, even when it hurts, is when God will start to move in our lives. We tend to want Him to move before we act. It is not enough to just say "God, just fix my life. Make it right, and blessed and fruitful." Have you ever seen fruit on a tree before it blossoms? An apple tree only bears fruit once it blossoms, and then and only then will the fruit begin to grow. It does something first. Abraham was called a friend of God because of his faith walk. This indicates that God enjoys it when we trust Him, when we have faith in Him. It's what He wants us to do. He wants us to be His friend.

James 2:26 says, *"For as the body without the spirit is dead; so faith without works is dead."* You know that you will die without your spirit; so it is with faith. Without your actions of trust and belief in God, it means nothing. You die spiritually.
I ask you to consider, "What kind of faith do you have?" **If** you know that you are lacking, act now. Show God that you truly love Him, trust Him, and believe in Him. Watch the blessings of God overtake you. You, too, can become His friend. You, too, can take the faith walk, and "Watch God Move."

✳

6

Unfruitful

"The worries of this life; the deceitfulness of wealth, and the desires for all these things, come in and choke the Word; making it unfruitful." Mark 4:19

The troubles we face from day to day become our primary focus. We become overwhelmed with work, car problems, money, children and college, where to go on vacation, housework, yard work, and making life-changing decisions. We seldom have time to do the thing that would be most beneficial to our relationship with God and produce the benefits of the Word of God in our lives. We make day to day living into a worry, rather than trust that God will care for us, and make a way out of no way. It's the desires we have that weigh us down and keep us from the victory God desires to give us. These desires overwhelm us so much, that it chokes the Word in us, which makes the Word unfruitful. In *Mark 4:19* Jesus clearly explained what makes us unfruitful; producing no fruit of our faith walk. When you look at the word unfruitful, expand your thoughts to the many promises God has given us in His Word. He has promised many blessings—spiritual ones—as well as to make us prosperous. He has promised that we are healed by the blood that Jesus shed, and that we may lay lands on the sick and they shall recover. We are victorious and overcomers, as we have power and authority over the evil one. Also consider the fruits of the Spirit that should become who we are, and how we live on a daily basis. If we consider all of these as fruit we should be producing, then what's he problem? This scripture says it's the worries of his world, the deceitfulness of wealth, and the desires of all these things that come in and choke the Word, therefore making the Word you know and told dear unfruitful.

Doesn't it stand clearly understood that either there is faith and trust in God—totally, completely and entirely—or anything else is worry? We can't fret over the troubles in our lives or even the simple matters because it becomes worry.

Recently, as I needed to make an important decision in my life, God helped me to understand that my thinking about, considering different options, and constantly trying to determine the best approach was a form of worry. I had a decision to make about my future, as the opportunity came to leave the company for which I had worked more than 34 years. My department had been approached and offered a lay-off package for two or three positions in our group. With this offer, they clearly stated the options we had, and that if they didn't get enough volunteers they would have to make the selection. When the desired qualifications were read that would be used to determine who would not be considered, I had those qualifications. So the decision to leave wasn't going to be an easy one, and it appeared they weren't going to do it for me. So in the natural there was nothing to consider because who in their right mind would leave a perfectly good job? Just thank God and move on.

However, I had a desire to be able to do more for the glory of God and a full-time job just didn't allow it. I was a few years from early retirement and the package offered would almost take me to that age. For several years I had been praying to be able to leave by age 52 and work full time for God, but due to some financial obligations, I felt it better to wait it out until 55. As hard as I tried to place this package offer out of my mind and move on, it kept coming up. Everywhere I turned, it seemed I was hearing it's time to do what God has called you to do. He will take care of you. These words were coming from those who did not realize the opportunity I was facing.

We had been given a few weeks to consider, and were given a final date to volunteer. I found myself writing down numbers and trying to determine how financially benefit, what to payoff, how to make it work, and not have worries and concerns from a financial standpoint. Each time I thought I had resolved to stay and not leave, something else or someone would say something that would leave a thought in the back of my mind.

Eventually, I became confused and I knew that God was not the author of confusion. I had been constantly praying and seeking God, but at this point I realized I had allowed the evil one to come and bring confusion. I had made my trusting relationship with God into lack of trust. I had made this situation into a worry of this life. I desired to create a peaceful situation of comfort; knowing that I was going to have more than enough money for retirement by trusting more in the company I worked for than God. I knew the Word of God. I knew God said that He would care for me, bless me, watch over me, and that I was a joint heir with Jesus. I had taught it many times.

I had the right to everything that God had promised... **It** was mine... Yet, here I was, overcome by a concern. I had let a care of this world overtake me. It wasn't until reading this scripture that I realized that the deceitfulness of what money can do creates false hopes and sways us to choose comfortable decisions to avoid future problems that might occur by only having just enough money.

I began my prayer that morning telling God how much I trusted Him to work out this situation and to direct my path. It was then that God spoke deep into my spirit, "why do you worry?" I began to state my case to God explaining that I was not worried because I knew I could make it either way. To stay would allow me to create a more than enough retirement, while leaving now would mean that I would have just enough. But I wanted to choose the direction that He desired for me and I needed His help in doing so.

The more I explained, the more I realized, I was a worrier. I began thinking back to other times I had to make decisions and had made it a time of worry. This had become a personality trait that I thought was a benefit because I was the kind of person that always took the time to think things through thoroughly. It sometimes kept me from sleeping, and consumed my thoughts while I was awake.

I thought this trait kept me from making swift foolish decisions. It was then that I realized I had been wrong and I immediately asked God to forgive and help me to give Him my life and allow Him to truly direct my path. I gave the matter to Him and refused to pick it up again. I told God if He wanted me to accept this opportunity to let me know, otherwise I was going to work and be a blessing on the job as opportunities were presented. I stopped putting numbers on paper. I stopped pondering over what others might think. I stopped carrying the package offer around in my briefcase and I refused to look at it during my lunch. I stopped trying to get others' opinions of what they thought. I gave it to God and moved on.

My last date to make the decision and turn in a signed form was on Monday, November 4, 2002. It was now November 1, and I had just been given a new assignment to work on a project with an implementation date of around March 2003. I dug into the project work that day as if I already knew my direction; resting in the fact that I had not heard from God and continued to trust in Him; giving it no more thought. On Sunday morning, November 3, 2002 the Lord spoke to my heart from the pulpit. It was clear and powerful; a Rhema Word from the Lord, as my pastor allowed God to use him. I knew without a doubt what God was saying to do.

We are all neatly wrapped up in our past accomplishments that we fail to see where

God is taking us, because we are always looking back at what we've done. This creates a false sense of security. So we hold on to what we know rather than simply trust God for where we are going.

It became so clear in my spirit that I had no doubt that God was saying, "trust me". I could hear Him saying, "It's time to move on." That Monday, November 4, 2002, I faxed my signed acceptance to the package I had been offered. My last day would officially be December 31, 2002.

I wanted to be able to see the end because I had concerns and worries of this life-my future. I was trusting in my monthly paycheck and the desires that it could provide for me if I continued to work and save enough so that I could live better than just comfortably. My desire was to live above where I was presently, and to have more than enough in the future. It was my desire over God's desire.

I was also looking at my accomplishments in the job that I had. I used these successes to try to determine my future and finding peace in what I could accomplish in the future with my house paid off, income from other sources as well as my IRA and my retirement savings from the company. I was looking for peace in knowing that I wouldn't have to live on just enough money and could go and come as I pleased. I was living *Mark 4:19*. It was the worries of this life and the deceitfulness of wealth and the desire for other things that choked out the word that I knew and loved; making the Word that was in me unfruitful.

The Word was supposed to be my comfort as God would direct my path. I couldn't hear God because of all my concerns and thoughts about my future. Yes my future was in God, but it was filled with my desires of what the flesh saw as comfort and peace. I was about to create an unfruitful life in Christ by making decisions based upon what makes sense in the natural, and what I desired, which would automatically make the Word bear no fruit, because I was trusting in the world's way of doing things.

I write this chapter from my home after having accepted the package offer. I am reminded of *Hebrews 11:8*. *"By faith Abraham, when called to go to a place he would later receive as his inheritance; obeyed and went even though he did not know where he was going."* It is important to have a relationship with God that you can hear Him speak.

It is not important to know the end; but that you trust Him enough to walk with Him to lead and direct you to the place where you are going. That kind of relationship cannot exist when you are overcome by worry, discouragement, and fear. All these emotions will choke out the word, putting you on a vicious circle of confusion. Remember, where there is confusion lays the deceptiveness of the evil one, who desires you not to hear from God; who desires you not to trust in Him and desires to keep you unfruitful.

How faithful is my God at answering prayer? I left Duke at the age of 52. The thing that makes me laugh is that my last day with the company was December 31, 2002. On January 10, 2003 I turned 53. I thought about my prayers concerning leaving, and I never said, "Pay my bills so I can leave at 52." I just said, "I want to be able to leave at 52, and work for the Lord." To be debt-free was a separate prayer statement, which I thought would get me ready so I could retire at 52.

I can't help but laugh when I think of how faithful God is to His Word and how I can trust Him to answer my prayers. You just have to be specific in how you pray, or it may not be exactly what you meant to say. However humorous my answer, I know I can trust Him to be faithful in answering my debt freedom. My prayer to work for God full time has also been answered as I am now employed by a world known Christian ministry that opens the door for me to talk with and pray for many. Isn't that just like God?

Every day, as Christians, we are required to trust God. In this life-changing event, I initially portrayed all the characteristics of someone who doesn't trust in God. I had already written many of the previous chapters, talked about faith in God and being overcome by worry, stress, fear, and discouragement; yet I possessed **all** of these during this particular event in my life. With each breath we take we must place our lives in God's hand or we risk getting off track and missing what God has for us; and most of all becoming unfruitful.

✻

7

Focused on the Wrong Thing

Whom have I in heaven but Thee? And besides thee, I desire nothing on earth." **Psalm 73:25**

One major thing that seems to weight us down as Christians is our natural ability to stay focused on the wrong things. It is an innocent but toxic problem to gaining Godly results. We don't consider it worry or anxiety, but just our way of bringing to reality our heart's desire. We focus on the house, the car, or the clothes we desire to buy. We've got pictures of what we want them to look like. 'We daydream about our wedding day, and have it all planned out but haven't a clue who we are marrying. We've been told that it's okay to keep those things as desires of our heart, but most of us don't know how to separate desires of hearts from turning those desires into worries, and in some cases, gods.

We complicate our life with these type worries because when they don't come to pass in our time, we get frustrated and sometimes depressed. Could that be the reason the Word says "Take no thought to what tomorrow may hold, because the same God that takes care of the birds can surely take care of you."? If we keep our mind stayed on Him, there is no time to focus on worldly desires. Even though these desires are not sins, we give so much attention to them that they become our primary focus and reason that we serve God. We will travel from conference to conference trying to find out what we need to do in order to bring our desire to pass. We make confessions and pay money for a Godly purpose hoping that this will begin the deliverance of our desire.

David writes in *Psalm 73:25, "Besides thee, I desire nothing on earth.".* Doing it God's way simply means there is more time to focus on Him than on the worldly desires. There is more time to meditate on His Word and become the obedient child He desires you to be. The more time we spend with Him, the less we are frustrated, worried or concerned with the cares of this world.

As we know more of Him, we often find that those things we desired will become minor to us, which allows God to become our provider.

Hebrews 12:2 says, *"Let us fix our eyes on Jesus, the author of our faith, who for the joy set before him endured the cross, scorning its shame, and sat down at the right hand of the throne of God."* If we take our eyes off God we get distracted by our surrounding circumstances and lose focus on the one that is most important. Jesus was the perfect example of staying focused. He knew what was before Him, so He endured the unpleasant and scornful actions placed upon Him—even to the cross. It was after what He endured that He was able to sit down at the right hand of the throne of God. He stayed focused; so that you would not grow weary and lose heart with the trials that you face from day to day. Jesus knows that we can do it, if we will just trust God.

The Christian walk involves some tough work, as we give up any and all that interfere with our relationship with God. To be an effective Christian, we must keep our eyes on Jesus. Our suffering and trials are many times the training ground that moves us to our God-appointed destiny.

We spend entirely too much time focusing on our disappointments and troubles; therefore, our hearts and minds are not fixed on Jesus. We spend hours talking to others about what someone has done or didn't do. We talk about the fact that prayer is out of the schools, and they want to take "In God We Trust" *off* the money. As disappointing as these actions might be, they are distractions set by the enemy. What we should be talking about is what God is doing, and can do. He can put prayer back in the school through children who love Him and are committed to His service, and through children who realize they cannot complete a day without prayer in their life.

Regardless of the words "In God We Trust" being on our money, God doesn't need that to show that He has people who trust Him. What He does need is you to trust Him, depend on Him, and stay focused on Him and Him only. He needs each Christian to demonstrate that they are an over- comer despite what they take out of the school, or take off the money. If God wants his name on the money there is no demon in hell that can move it. The action for us is to stay focused on God and do what He is telling us to do. Yes, we may have missed a great opportunity to keep prayer officially in school, but that was yesterday and now we must move on, or we will miss another opportunity to be obedient to His command. If prayer was taken out of the schools, it was because we were not focused on what God was saying to us. It is important to stay focused and alert to what God is saying because God doesn't lose battles; we give the battle away.

Luke 24:36-47

36) While they were still talking about this, Jesus himself stood among them and said to them, "peace be with you".
37) They were startled and frightened, thinking they saw a ghost.
38) He said to them, "Why are you troubled, and why do doubts rise in your minds?"
39) Look at my hands and feet. It is I myself! Touch me and see; a ghost does not have flesh and bones, as you see I have."
40) When he had said this, he showed them his hands and feet.
41) and while they still did not believe it because of joy and amazement, he asked them, "Do you have anything here to eat?"
42) They gave him a piece of broiled fish,

43) *And he took it and ate it in their presence.*

44) *He said to them, "This is what I told you while I was still with you: Everything must be fulfilled that is written about me in the Law of Moses, the Prophets and the Psalms.*

45) *Then he opened their minds so they could understand the Scriptures.*

46) *He told them, "This is what is written: The Christ will suffer and rise from the dead on the third day,*

47) *And repentance and forgiveness of sins will be preached in his name to all nations, beginning at Jerusalem.*

We need to keep our focus on our purpose as children of The Most High. We have a mission and many have lost focus of what He said just before He went up to heaven. Christ questioned them and wanted to know why they were so troubled. Just as I think He is asking us today, . "Have you forgotten what I did?" Have you forgotten everything I said? Have you lost focus?

Jesus recognized that they had lost focus because they were discussing all the horrible things that had taken place at the cross. Jesus takes the time to remind them of their purpose. He tells them that repentance and forgiveness of sins will be preached in His name to all nations, beginning with Jerusalem. He opened their minds to understand the scriptures because it had already been written, but they had lost focus and had become confused and troubled by the events that had taken place. Have we forgotten that He said repentance and forgiveness of sins will be preached in His name to all nations? As children of God we have a responsibility to tell somebody about the goodness of God; that He loves us and forgives all who will repent of their sins.

Much to my regret, we will be like the disciples if we continue to watch what Satan is doing: He will use situations to make us think we are defeated. God is saying, "fix your eyes on Jesus, the author and finisher of our faith. To stay focused, you must first be able to trust in God, or the circumstances that surround you will seem bigger than God, causing you to miss the victory. The disciples missed the victory at the cross. They could only see the bad and became discouraged. They found themselves sitting around talking about what Satan had done.

If you will stay focused and remember *"He is able to do exceedingly, abundantly, above all we could ever ask or think." (Ephesians 3:20)*, you will see the victory that belongs to you. So while we are talking about what Satan has done; we could be trusting in what God is going to do, until your victory is won.

✳

8

It Is Finished!

When He had received of the drink, Jesus said, "It is finished". With that, He bowed his head and gave up His Spirit. John 19:30

After taking the time to understand what really took place with the death of Jesus, in simple terms, there is no reason to not trust God. As I began to prepare a message during the "Easter Holidays of 2003", I became overwhelmingly aware that God wanted me to connect what His death did on the cross—as He sacrificed His life for us—with why we should be able to trust Him. It is important to realize that because God has sacrificed it all for us, without a shadow of doubt, He can be trusted. If God gave His one and only Son for us, why would He be anything less than trustworthy? Who do you know that would give that much, and not be there for you during difficult times? Why would He suffer so much? Why would He take the punishment, the pain and anguish? Why? Because He loves us so much that He would give it all, so that we might be victorious through Christ Jesus, His Son. The word here is victorious. To be victorious through what He has done, we must trust what the cross did for us. To stop now and not be there for us at this point, would make the events of the cross a waste. The cross should show us He is committed to His Word.

Jesus, God's only son, was sent to earth for a mission; a destiny. It was clearly what I would refer to as a "Mission Accomplished." Jesus stated it so clearly just before dying on the cross with his words, *"It is finished."* The word finished implies or represents "complete, over, nothing left to do; to bring something to an end." Jesus was saying that all He had come to do had been accomplished.

His coming and purpose had been prophesied throughout Isaiah. God had sent His only Son to earth on a mission that would be remembered throughout the ages. He would come to earth and be the living Word; God in the flesh. He would suffer at the hand of man a horrible death, but gain the victory to the Glory of His Father with the resurrection. It was then that I realized that anyone who would do this for me can be trusted with the minor events of my life.

Jesus took the sins of this world to the grave and He did it for us. He remained focused on His purpose even as He hung on the cross forgiving one of the robbers. He had to be forsaken by His Father in order for this to take place; because if God had not stepped back to allow this horrible death, Satan couldn't have touched Him. He was laughed at, mocked, criticized, beat, slapped, whipped, kicked, wore a crown of thorns, pierced in the side and hung on a cross to die a sinners death. Why? All so that we might have a right to the tree of life; all so that He could give life and give it more abundantly, to defeat the very one that wanted Him destroyed, and so that we may become joint heirs with Him. What belongs to Jesus now also belongs to us. We are joint heirs with Him. That is reason enough to lay down all concern and doubt, and just praise His name.

Isaiah 53:4-5 (Amplified Bible)
> *Surely he has borne our grief's (sicknesses, weaknesses, and distresses) and carried our sorrows and pains (of punishment), yet we (ignorantly) considered Him stricken, smitten, and afflicted by*

God (as if with leprosy). But He was wounded for our transgressions.

He was bruised for our guilt and iniquities; the chastisement (needful to obtain) peace and well-being for us was upon Him, and the stripes (that wounded) Him we are healed and made whole.

If Jesus were standing before you today, he could say:

1. I took the stripes upon my back, now you are healed.
2. The shedding of my blood; now no more sacrifices of lambs.
3. I was wounded for your transgressions and your sins; now you can live free from sin.
4. I bore your weaknesses; now you can be strong because of what I did.
5. For every pain I took upon my body, for every time they spit on me, laughed at me, mocked me, criticized me; I carried your sorrows, pains and punishment so that you could have victory.
6. I took bruises upon my body for your iniquities, wickedness and sins; so that

you can be an overcomer and joint heir with me.

7. I did this so that you could be free of sin. I came to give life and give it more abundantly.

8. I came so that you might have a right to the tree of life.

9. I came to be a living sacrifice.

10. I came to die for you, so that my mission would be complete-to defeat Satan.

11. I came to be an example.

12. I came so that you would know that you could trust my Father. ,

13. I did all this so you would know how much I love you.

14. I came and completed my purpose and destiny. It is finished I gave up the ghost.

15. I came to bury the sinful past of every child of God.

16. Satan, you couldn't take my life, I gave my life. So now my joint heirs are victorious because my work was completed. My Mission was Accomplished; It was Finished.

My Christian friends, because of what Jesus did for you, you don't have to look back, stress out about your past, worry, fret, gossip and have anxiety over what's going on in this world today-it is finished. His mission was completed over 2000 years ago when He said, "It is finished." This means that when Satan tries to remind you of your past, or anything that will take away your faith and trust in God, tell him, "It is finished."

Realizing it was finished on Calvary increased my trust in God to take care of me no matter what the situation. I have resolved to not allow anything past, present, or future to get in the way of my faith in God. If His Word says it, then I trust that it is so. No matter what it looks like, or feels like, God will bring me through.

This brings to memory so clearly an accident some years back that my two teenage children, Larry and Michelle were involved in. Larry was seventeen and Michelle was fourteen when this life changing event took place. I arrived home from work to find my son's wrecked vehicle in the driveway. I remember feeling like it was a dream and not really understanding what I was looking at. The vehicle was demolished. The only way I determined that it was my son's car was by the license tag number. I ran into my home calling out their names to find that no one was home. I could feel my heart racing as if it were coming out of my chest. I immediately called my sister, Evone, who lived a few houses from me. I remember the cautiousness of the individual who answered the phone and heard my voice. At that moment my mind went blank as they explained that both of my children had been taken to the hospital. Despite all effort to keep me calm, I knew that something was extremely wrong; they had not just taken them to the hospital for minor injuries. At that very moment it was as if time stood still.

Arriving at the hospital, after a ride that seemed to take an eternity, I had to wait the dreaded time until they had finished the examinations. Finally, two doctors appeared to tell me that Michelle had received a severe concussion and had a blood clot in her left leg. They would release her to go home, but she would not be able to walk for about four weeks because of the blood clot. They would first treat her concussion and after the first week, she would return to the doctor, and they would begin treating the blood clot. The concussion was over her left eye, so the expectations were set for black and blue bruises on her face and possibly two black eyes.

They wrapped her leg tightly and once the week had passed, I was to return her to the hospital where they would check the blood clot that was the size of a quarter, and give her medication to prevent it from moving up to her heart. The precaution was based on the fact that the clot could move up to her heart before she returned, but they could not treat the clot and the concussion at the same time. The only hope they could give me was to be very careful and make sure she didn't walk on it for the entire four weeks, and especially before they could start treating it.

Then they began to discuss my son's situation. I was told that he had internal bleeding and that they had been unable to determine where the bleeding was in order to do surgery. The doctor so calmly explained that all of his injuries were internal and his last words were, "he probably will not survive." As they both looked at me to determine my state of mind, they asked the question to make sure they had been clear: "do you understand?" My reply was "Yes," but followed with "what are you trying to say?"

I think I understood, but felt this couldn't be real. They explained again, but with more detailed clarity, as they stated "he could die." They carefully informed me that when there is internal bleeding such as his, they usually cannot locate the injury in order to do the repairs. They calmly explained they would continue to work with him and return later to let us know if anything changed, but not much hope was given.

I turned to my family that had been waiting there with me to see faces of shock. We had **all** been silently praying for God to intervene. Then we were faced with the opportunity to trust and believe or doubt and forget everything we knew and supposedly believed in God's Word. There wasn't much talking, just looks of confusion and prayers. I knew that we were all fighting to keep the faith and trust in God. It went without saying, because that was all we had to trust in. Anything else and what the doctor's said would become real. So without really saying it, we didn't close the chapter on Larry's life. We kept the faith in our God.

In what seemed to be an eternity, the doctors returned with expressions of confusion on their face. They explained that Michelle would be ready to leave the hospital in a few minutes and then came the news. Larry's internal bleeding had stopped, and they didn't understand why. They still didn't know where it was coming from and had done nothing to stop it. It had stopped all by itself. The worst news they gave me was that he would not be able to walk for eight weeks and would have to lie in bed during that period, because his pelvic bones had been crushed. They didn't recommend a body cast as the best method of recovery, unless I felt that he would not stay in the bed for the period of time required. I put a big smile on my face and said, "It's the bed for eight weeks".

To share this story is to show you how much we can trust God. God didn't stop at just saving their lives. The next morning, as I was told to expect black eyes, and bruises on Michelle face; I was stunned to find her face clear and without any marks, scars, or head injury. A week later I took her to the doctor and they couldn't find the blood clot that was the size of a quarter, and which could have taken her life at any moment. The doctor looked confused as he explained she was free to walk out of the hospital—no wheelchair and no crutches. Michelle had experienced complete healing.

If that wasn't enough, four weeks later I took Larry to the doctor to see how well his crushed pelvic bones were healing. He had faithfully remained in his bed, and had not felt any pain during the entire time. The doctor walked in the room after reviewing the new x-rays and explained that the breaks were gone. The breaks had been there, he assured me, but for some reason had healed much faster than they had anticipated. Even though they couldn't locate the breaks, they felt it would be safest if he used crutches for the next two weeks. I agreed and the individual who had been carried in on a stretcher, now walked out of the doctor's office on his own.

Before returning home we picked up some crutches so that Larry could follow the doctor's orders. That evening I had choir practice and Larry was excited to go with me and be able to get out of the house. Next door to the church his cousin was playing basketball with some friends. Larry asked if he could go over and watch them play. I then expressed that he was not to play, but only watch. Two hours later I come out of the church shocked to find my son on the court playing basketball. As I looked I could not believe my eyes. From that point on, if the crutches were used, it was more of a precaution than a necessity. Within a few days he stopped using them all together. My God had once again shown His greatness. He went beyond what I could even imagine or think. I prayed for their recovery and God exceeded my thoughts of what I was expecting. He made sure that no individual could take credit for what He did. He worked a miracle.

Perhaps it didn't stop there. Larry had been examined several years before the accident and had needed to wear glasses for reading only. Wearing glasses wasn't exactly what he looked forward to each day, so as time passed, he stopped wearing them because he could get by without them. The accident was a result of him pulling in front of a car that was traveling about 70 MPH that hit him directly in his door. I questioned if maybe his eye sight had become worse, and that maybe he needed to wear glasses for driving since his eye problem was hereditary and usually got worse with age. So I took him to the optometrist to find that his eye sight was perfect. He no longer needed eye glasses for reading. I don't know if for some strange reason he grew out of the problem or if it was immediate divine intervention, but regardless, it is God who heals.

Larry is now 32, and Michelle is now 29. I can say this unpleasant but memorable event increased my trust and faith in God. When God does something, He finishes the job. Actually, it was finished over 2000 years ago when Jesus died on the cross for me, for my son and daughter, and for you.

✳

9

Why are we often defeated?

If ye abide in me, and my word abides in you, ye shall ask what ye will, and it shall be done unto you. John 15:7

Let me ask you a few questions. What is on your mind? What is in your heart? The answer that you give to these questions might be the answer to your success or defeat.

The above scripture indicates very clearly that we must abide. What does the word abide mean by Webster's definition?

Abide: *(1) to remain; continue; stay. (2) To dwell; reside. (3) To continue in a particular condition, attitude, relationship. (4) To wait for; await; (5) to endure, tolerate, sustain or withstand. (6) To accept without opposition or question. (7) To pay the price or penalty of; (8) to act in accord with; to submit to; agree to. To remain steadfast or faithful to.*

Abide is a small word that means so much. Any of the above describes what God expects of us when we abide in Him. We are to stay focused on Him with a faithful attitude and relationship. We allow His thoughts to become our thoughts with any situation we are going through. We wait and while we wait we endure, tolerate, and sustain. We don't question Him, but we trust Him to watch over us as we submit to will. We remain steadfast, unmovable, always abiding in Him with no doubt, distrust, fear, murmuring or complaining. We abide in Him with His word abiding in us.

Now the interesting thing is if His word is to abide in us, then it must remain in us continually. It must reside in us, establishing an attitude of trust and faith, while establishing a relationship with God, because we have faith in Him. We accept His word without opposition or question. We trust Him. Allowing His word to be steadfast in us, regardless the problem or trial we face. We are constantly thinking about Him and not the problem. We are often speaking His word, instead of talking about the problem. Instead of seeing the problem and our circumstance in the natural, we see ourselves as God sees us; victorious, blessed, joint heirs and overcomers in Christ Jesus. When we abide, we are fixed on Jesus.

Does this sound extreme? Maybe so, but go back and read that scripture again, then read the definition of abide. I think you will have to agree it is at the least what I have written, if not more. Why is it so hard for many of us to abide? To answer that question we will have to go back to the questions I initially asked. What's in your heart? What's on your mind? If it's anything but Christ and His word; then could it be that we are not abiding? We ask what we will, and expect it to be done unto us. This promise is based upon us abiding in Christ, and His word abiding in us. Reading His word twice a week, or attending that good church, or saying a scripture as a slogan for your situation won't necessarily bring you out victoriously. The scripture that you say has to be you. Who you are, and what you believe. It has to be what God has spoken to your spirit and not just words you quote from the Bible.

It has to be in your heart, rooted and grounded, steadfast and unmovable, always abiding. To quote a scripture, and it not be in your heart, rooted and grounded, is just to quote words with no power. It becomes just a slogan. It's the Word of God in your heart, and not just in your mind that will produce power and authority. God's Word is Powerful, but the heart of the one using it must abide in Christ.

We often do not abiding because we have so much other stuff in our heart, and mind. The Bible refers to it as the cares of this world. From TV soaps, talk shows, movies, our children, to simple day-to-day worry, are the things that occupy our hearts and minds. We only spend a small portion of our day with God, and when we do, it is often the last part of the day; just before we go to sleep. The day is spent concentrating on work, talking about some show we saw, worrying about what to do; or perhaps enjoying a good old complaining session about the events of the day. We are always trying to fix our problem or make things go the way we think they should. When all we need to do is abide in Him, with His word in our hearts, then we can ask what we will and it shall be given. The abiding God desires of us will create a trust in God that is unmovable.

I visited my daughter, Michelle, one weekend and found her to be completely different from the person I knew three weeks before who had been discouraged and troubled because of bills, and her job situation. She was living from paycheck to paycheck, and her job position could possibly come to an end at anytime. Her primary concern was the bills and how she would care for her son, Brandon.

Three weeks later I was talking to someone who seemed to have a glow about her, and confidence in who she is in Christ Jesus. When I mentioned money or her job, she spoke of them as either resolved, or as if they were minor concerns. She now seemed more focused on what God wanted her to do, and what she had been learning in The Word. I asked, "What caused the change in you?" She indicated she had spent hours reading, praying, and meditating. She even spent late nights praying and talking with God, and had began to abide in Him. The more she studied, the more His Word abided in her. The results were a noticeable, positive difference. She began to speak with power and authority over different problems in her life. The results were victory over many things she had been praying about for some time. She had begun to trust God in areas that she had not been able to before. Eventually she found a better job, and continues to be focused on what her call is in the body of Christ. There have been more trials and tribulations, but she learned the importance of abiding to bring you through.

You may have questions about my thoughts on abiding, and that's alright. However, I am sure you can learn something from this, even if you can't totally agree with me. Please understand one thing. These are not the words that I made up in my mind. It is exactly as God has begun to reveal Himself to me. The more I desire to know His will for my life, the more He reveals to me on abiding in Him and His Word abiding in me. I am resolved that I cannot look at my problems in the natural, but if I abide in Him and His Word abides in me, that I will see things differently than they are in the natural. I will see them as God sees them.

He wants to deliver us and provide for us. He doesn't want you to be defeated. All He wants is for us to abide, so that we will be able to walk by faith and not by sight. When you can walk hand in hand with God, you will develop a trust beyond what you can ever imagine in the natural.

You will overcome the doubt and disbelief that prevents you from asking God in faith. When you can ask God for your heart's desire with this type of confidence (faith, trust), you can move the heart of God and it shall be done unto you.

✳

č

10

Let It Go!

I suppose most of us at some point in our lives have something that we classify as important to us in this world. It may be our children, home, spouse, significant other, job, car, precious collections, organization, and the list could go on. Caring for something in this world is not a hard thing to do; it comes natural to most of us. Based upon our personalities and life styles, we become attached to different things.

I can remember when I was growing up most teenagers treasured their cars. They washed them and spoke of them as if they were human. Some have carried that habit on into their adult lives. For others it may have been the house they had always dreamed of. They planned, saved and wished for it night and day, until one day it was theirs and now they have to start planning on decorating it. Despite what we buy, we can always find more. Then there are those who cherish their loved ones above all else. Loving your family isn't what's bad;

but it is when you allow your family to become the center of your existence that creates the problem.

More complex than everything else I have mentioned is those who allow their church/ religious organization to become their god. Their focus becomes working at the church and doing those things that get them recognized as faithful church workers. This individual will often find it very difficult to let go of their position when someone else is elected in their place. What should be a simple transition turns into a nightmare and an all out carnal war. They decide to fight for their loved and admired position until the end. They can become overwhelmed with church work and playing the part. In time, their heart can so easily become hard and callus to the prompting of the Holy Spirit. Their church position becomes their god. As long as they are faithful to the work they are doing, they never stop to see what God is saying to them. They continue with their religious acts.

Let us examine what Paul writes in *Philippians 3:1-10, 12-17 (Amplified)*. I think his life can be an example for us.

> 6) As to my zeal; I was a persecutor of the church, and by the Law's standard of righteousness (supposed justice, up-rightness, and right standing with God) I was proven to be blameless and no fault was found with me.
>
> 7) But whatever former things I had that might have been gains to me. I have come to consider as loss for Christ sake.
>
> 8) Yes, furthermore, I count everything as loss compared to the possession of the priceless privilege (the overwhelming preciousness) the surpassing worth, and supreme advantage) of knowing Christ Jesus my Lord and of progressively becoming more deeply and intimately acquainted with Him (of perceiving and recognizing and understanding Him more fully and clearly). For His sake I have lost everything and consider it all to be mere rubbish (refuse, dregs) in order that I may win (gain) Christ (the Anointed One).
>
> 9) And that I may (actually) be found and known as in Him, not having any (self-achieved) righteousness that can be called my own, based on my obedience to the Law's demands (ritualistic uprightness and supposed right standing with God thus acquired), but possessing that (genuine righteousness) which comes through faith in Christ (the Anointed One), the (truly) right standing with God, which comes from God by (saving) faith.

10) (For my determined purpose is) that I may know Him (that I may progressively become more deeply and intimately acquainted with Him, perceiving and recognizing and understanding the wonders of His Person more strongly and more clearly), and that I may in that same way come to know the power outflowing from His resurrection (which exerts over believers), and that I may so share His sufferings as to be continually transformed (in spirit into His likeness even) to His death, (in the hope).

This is a powerful commitment made by a man who is completely sold out. In verses 7 and 8 Paul wants us to realize that nothing else matters but Christ. What he encourages us to do is let it all go and trust Christ. Paul considered everything unimportant compared to his relationship with Christ. I even think his comparison is so strong that we have to stop and consider where we are in our relationship with Christ. Paul refers to everything else as rubbish, refuse or dregs. All of which can be referred to as waste, garbage, trash or junk. That's a strong comparison that cannot be taken and pushed aside, so that you or I can make excuses about our love for other things.

Now look at how he esteems Christ. His words are just as strong but show value in his relationship with Christ. Paul sees his relationship with Christ as priceless, overwhelming preciousness; something he couldn't put a price on. When you hold anything as precious or priceless you will take extreme steps to protect that which you hold dear. A man with this type attitude will let nothing stand in his way. He will sacrifice it all to gain a true and intimate relationship with the (god) God he holds as priceless and overwhelmingly precious.

To know Him and obtain an intimate relationship with God, you must let go of the cares of this world. He is a jealous God and will have no other gods before Him. So one has to realize that it is not in the shiny cars, big homes, nice jobs, church positions, religious organization, or any other possession that will connect you with God, In fact your love for these things may hinder your relationship with Him.

Paul once persecuted the church, and was a Pharisee, acknowledging that all that he had done could not save him. He indicates that if anyone could be saved by what he has done it would have been him. Paul's testimonial was based upon how he persecuted the church for the sake of religion. Paul did what he did from his heart, but what he realized was that those things we do that are not in the will of God benefit nothing to our salvation, no matter how right we may think we are. All that Paul had done before and after his deliverance was worthless when compared with the priceless gain of knowing Christ Jesus. He put aside everything else, counting it worthless in order to have Christ.

The question must be asked, "Would you give up these things to gain a more intimate relationship with Him?" If you were prompted to sell your home and give the money to the poor, or to help a ministry that you knew was led by God, could you? What if you had to give up your position as Missionary President, Sunday School Teacher, Youth Leader, etc.— could you? Or would you harbor resentment and anger towards your replacement and those who supported them? Would you start a disagreement for the sake of making your point? What if someone wanted to change the order of service that had been in place for years, because they wanted to make the service meet the needs of others and not just a specific group? Would you find it worthwhile to argue your point and fight to have it remain the same as it had been for years—not giving any thought to those who may desire a more contemporary format; therefore taking a chance that they may leave, so you could remain happy?

How can you operate with the Holy Spirit when in fact you focus on yourself, your desires, your wants, and not the wants and the desires of the Holy Spirit? Romans 8:6-7 makes it very clear how a carnal mind will affect your relationship with God. *"For to be carnally minded is death; but to be spiritually minded is life and peace. Because the carnal mind is enmity (hostility, hate, antagonistic, opposition) against God....."* This says it all. It is not possible to have a trusting intimate relationship with God while we continue daily to operate with a carnal mind. If you think being hostile and antagonistic is not enough to separate you from the presence of the Holy Spirit, then surely being in opposition does. Paul's use of the word carnal implies a deep, seated animosity or hatred against the ways of God.

You like operating out of your flesh. You find operating out of the spirit frustrating, and resent loving your enemies and doing good to those who spitefully use you. You agonize over matters that cause you to change, give in or let go of your ways and desires. This enmity can only be changed through the redemptive power of God Himself if you will just let go and admit that you need to grow up and start eating meat from the spiritual table of God.

"Letting go" means you must die to your flesh and its wants. When you die, you will be able to trust God completely, because you will rely upon Him totally.

To have the attitude that Paul had means you have a complete and total trust in God. You are fighting the good fight of faith. You see and understand that your success and trust are not in earthly things, but rest in God alone. *Philippians 3:3*, Paul says he has no confidence in the flesh because we worship god in the Spirit. We can have no confidence in what we do out of our flesh, but only in those things prompted by the Spirit of God. Our relationship with God is established in the Spirit.

The next time you are in a church meeting and someone mentions doing away with something that you hold dear, check your heart. Is there scriptural support for keeping it, or is it just dear to your heart and what you have become accustomed to?

This death that Paul experienced allowed him to be content sitting in a Roman jailor stranded on an island. No matter what was about to happen to Paul or what he was going through, Paul was content. He was content in doing the work of the Father. He was content to be able to write letters from jail. He was not moved by His circum- stances because he had let go of his cares and his life was truly in the hands of God.

> 12) Not that I have now attained (this ideal), or have already been made perfect, but I press on to lay hold of (grasp) and make my own, that for which Christ Jesus (the Messiah) has laid hold of me and made me His own.
> 13) I do not consider, brethren, that I have captured and made it my own (yet); but one thing I do (it is my one aspiration) forgetting what lies ahead.

14) I press on toward the goal to win the (supreme and heavenly) prize to which God in Christ Jesus is calling us upward:
15) So let those (of us) who are spiritually mature and full-grown have this mind and hold these convictions and if in any respect you have a different attitude of mind; God will make that clear to you also.
16) Only let us hold true to what we have already attained and walk and order our lives by that.
17) Brethren, together follow my example and observe those who live after the pattern we have set for you.

Paul, who was a natural man, was dead to this world but treasured his relationship with God. He recognized and admits that he had to keep moving towards where God would have him to be because he has not completed the journey. The amplified uses the words *straining forward* in verse 13 that catches my attention and indicates that it will take effort to keep pressing forward. He is working or pressing daily to reach the mark for the prize that is set before him. He is keeping His eyes on God and nothing else matters as he brings all his energy toward this purpose. Take note that it is a daily effort.

It is important to recognize and understand what Paul says in verse 15. To take on this attitude of pressing forward, he speaks to those of us that are spiritually mature and full grown to have this same mind. His instructions are to the mature in Christ to press and strain forward to what lies ahead. Could it be that those who are not mature in Christ will not have the mind to go through the pressing and the straining on a daily basis? Those who are not mature may not be willing to make the effort because their heart and mind will be more directed towards their needs and wants. To press as Paul indicates requires that one be dead to their own desires and wants and have sold out totally to Christ. He says very clearly that those of us who are spiritually mature and full grown are to have this same mind as He had. His encouragement was to consider everything else as worthless and unimportant, and consider the things of God as precious over all else. This reminds me of the Words spoken by Paul in *Philippians 1:21* when he says *"to die is gain"*.

Paul encourages us to seek God for understanding if our opinion on the subject is different. Relying on God is important and not a man inspired opinion to avoid continued confusion on the subject. If you depend on God to reveal these things to you but you will not let go of your carnal attitude and continue to act from your flesh and not the Spirit, God will not open your eyes to these things. You will spend more time looking for a way to hold on to your car, home, and possessions rather than freely letting go.

The phrase I am most familiar with that people often say is, "I don't see anything wrong with this." That statement could be right if the car is just a car to you, or if the TV is just a TV. There isn't anything wrong because He loves to give us nice things, and He wants us to work for Him, but it is wrong to put them before God. It is wrong to worship it. It is wrong to esteem anything higher than your commitment to God—yes, even your adored church position and your opinion of a situation. To understand and move with the Spirit of God, we must keep our hearts open to God so that He can move about freely in us. Look at it this way. You invite God into your home to stay and tell Him to make Himself at home.

Doing this is somewhat different from letting in the average person and making that statement. To the average person you invite to your home to stay, this means move about the specified areas freely, get yourself water, soda, and food from the refrigerator or pantry. This person can get up and retire to bed when they want to, but there are some things they can't do. They can't move your furniture around, change the carpet or the color of your walls, tell you when to rise or when to rest, or bring in new pieces of furniture as they desire.

This is how many of us treat God when we have invited Him in to stay. You can do all those normal things and those things that I am comfortable with and accustomed to, but every- thing else is off limits. This is not how God wants it to be. He wants to be able to move about freely, moving whatever furniture He desires, when He wants to move it, as well as changing things around. He wants access to every corner and area of your heart.

It is not easy to let someone have this type of control of our lives, but it is what we have to do if we want to develop a trust with God above what we could ever imagine in the natural. Once we let Him move things, change things and show us through trust what He can do, our lives will never be the same; but to experience this we must let go of all that we hold precious in our lives.

Verse 16 Paul's encouragement was to walk in what they had already obtained, and live their lives by that. Why do something different when you already know what works or pleases God? It reminds me of an athlete who has worked hard and obtains victory at some level. The next challenge would be to move past the obtained level of victory onto the next level. To do that, you don't stop doing what you already know works. You start there and move forward to obtain and receive victory at a new level. So there is no need in looking back, but pushing forward with God as our guide. Don't find yourself repeating old sins or going back to old habits you have been delivered from—walk forward with God by your side.

Now last, in verse 17, Paul says look at me, watch me, and do as I have done; let me be an example. Why? As mentioned in verse 6, he had once operated out of his flesh and now had totally turned his life over to God. He had once thought that he was doing it right, and did it to the fullest and now was doing the same with God as His guide. Paul persecuted the Christian and was feared throughout the Christian community. He thought that he was doing what was right, so he did not half-do the job. Later Paul, after his experience on the road to Damascus, *(Acts 9:3-19)* began to preach Christ as the Son of God. This change put his life in danger many times, but without looking back, Paul pressed forward towards the prize.

Christ was the greatest example of being dead to this world, but because He was the Son of God, many of us cannot relate, or we see Him as above us as He was; but that we can never obtain the attitude in which He became so selfless. It is so easy for us to say scripture and sing songs about being like Jesus. We say it, and sing it, but many never take on the real desire from their heart to do it.

The question remains, "Are you holding on to something?" If the answer is yes, then let it go. It's amazing how much closer your relationship with the father will become. It is so awesome how you will be able to trust God when there are no carnal actions, attitudes, or thoughts to hinder your connection. What you must realize is that when you are holding on to something above God, you will have more confidence and trust in the thing you hold dear. Once that thing has been let go, God can fill that spot. The more He is able to fill you with his ways and desires, the closer you become to Him and the more you will trust Him.

It goes without saying, that you trust something or in something. The question is, will you admit where you are, so that you can enjoy a closer walk with the Lord? Will you continue to hold on to what has kept you from trusting God completely?

"Letting go" means you are ready to eat meat, and don't want to continue being fed milk. You are now ready to operate with the Holy Spirit and not out of your carnal desires. Letting go is complete and total trust in God. You have basically acknowledged that you no longer want to do it your way, but you want to do it God's way, which makes you a living sacrifice. It may mean acknowledging that the issue you have with your church or pastor is in fact a carnal issue, and not spiritual. It may mean acknowledging that you have to lay all your church positions before God and ask Him to show you the purpose you were made for. It may require you showing love to someone who isn't lovable by natural terms. It may require you to show appreciation and love to that husband that in the natural gets on your last nerve. It may mean change. The end result is trust in a God that can deliver you out of every situation you are facing today.

＊

"Resting in the Presence of God"

Blessed is the man who trusts in the LORD and whose trust is the LORD. For he will be like a tree planted by the water, that extends its roots by a stream and will not fear when the heat comes; but its leaves will be green and it will not be anxious in a year of drought nor cease to yield fruit. **Jeremiah 17:7,8**

Blessed is the man who trusts in the Lord and whose trust is the Lord's. What a powerful and commanding statement to end on. Many people know of God. Many have experiences where they know God worked out a problem, or answered a prayer, but who is the man that really knows God and can honestly say that their trust is God? My trust is not in what I see or what I touch. My trust is not in having money, a job, or anything in the natural. My trust is only In God and Him alone.

To develop this kind of trust, one must rest in God completely. Rest implies that you can relax regardless of your situation, trial, tribulation or problem. You are not swayed to worry, fret, stress out and be discouraged over anything that life presents. Your trust is in the Lord and not in the outcome of your problem because you know that God will bring you out. You know that if He doesn't bring you out, the victory is not based upon the outcome, but the glory belongs to God.

It becomes like Esther's attitude *(Esther 4:16)*: *"if I perish, let me perish,"* because God's desire is more important than mine. This attitude towards your situation puts you in the presence of God and He will begin to guide and direct your life. You will be set up to be blessed. When the attitude of the individual is directed towards God and His desire, God recognizes that this person is planted in faith and trust. Then the power of God will become real to the individual and the blessings will overflow.

If you are still trying to handle your problems in the natural, you are not resting. If you continue to find yourself frustrated and anxious over life, you are not resting. If you find yourself offended and angry over persecution that comes for righteousness sake *(St. Matthew 5:10)*, you are not resting in the presence of God.

To rest in the presence of God is to know His love. The Bible refers to it as the fullness of God. *Ephesians 3:19* says, *"To know the love of Christ which passes knowledge that you may be filled with all the fullness of God."* To know Him is not based upon what you think about Him, but what you have experienced with Him. It is a heart condition based upon intimacy with Him. God desires to fill you with the Holy Spirit; to fill you with His presence, and this fullness is only obtained through intimacy with Him. It is the Holy Spirit's responsibility to bring it to pass once we begin to trust—despite our problems. His love will begin to grow in us, filling us with His presence.

Getting to know God is like the quality relationships we establish in the natural. Two people meet, but the true relationship is not sealed until they establish a relationship with each other by spending time together. It requires them to talk and listen. Initially, there may be some feelings of doubt and lack of trust. As time goes on, if the relationship is to continue, a trust is developed. They both can begin to make statements about each other's likes and dislikes. They may even adjust their life in someway to show respect for each other in the area of their likes and dislikes. As time passes, they are able to rest in peace about their relationship because they will know that the other cares for them. They honestly believe and know that the friend will not harm them in any way. They begin to relax. They begin to rest in that person's trust. That's what we need to do with God. Spend time with Him; get to know Him by reading His Word, praying and fasting, and listening for His voice. Do what His Word says because God honors His Word.

Many times we get saved and dedicate our lives to God. We immediately start to make plans about our relationship with him. We start by saying how much we love him, and care about Him, yet we really don't know anything about Him. We haven't read the Word. We've practically spent very little time praying and meditating. We speak Words we hear others say about Him. We talk of His love, which is real and is there, but we don't know Him. So we don't rest in His promises. We are overburdened with worry and frustration because we really don't know Him. We find ourselves in church business meetings, choir practice, or a fellowship meeting arguing and trying to make our point. Trying to make others see it our way or make others change. We don't really realize that we can trust God to handle all our problems — yes even in our meetings and fellowships. At this point we are in a place to begin trusting God and establishing a wonderful relationship with Him. The sad thing is that's where many of us stay for years. Some never make it past this point — stuck in a circle of confusion and never moving to a mature trust of faith in God.

God wants us to develop a relationship with Him. He wants us to seek to know Him and understand His ways. *Matthew 6:33* **says,** *"Seek ye first the kingdom of God, and His righteousness, and all these things shall be added to you."* He wants to show Himself mightily to each of us, if we will just spend time seeking Him-not the fame, fortune or recognition, but time spent getting to know Him. Many wait to seek Him in the moment or time of crisis, and that's alright. The ultimate commitment would be to establish that wonderful relationship before the dark moment appears in your life.

Wouldn't it be good to know that you are "RESTING IN GOD'S PRESENCE," no matter what storms may hail? Only then will we know of *the peace that surpasses all understanding (Philippians 4:7).*

The real remedy for your fear, worry, stress, anxiety, and discouragement is resting in God. His peace exceeds anything your natural mind can understand. In the natural this won't make sense, but through an intimate relationship with God, you will know that you can rest. God's Word is true. He is able to do all that He says he will do for us, but we have to seek Him. We need to establish that trusting relationship with Him and be filled with His presence. That's the only way we will ever be found resting in His presence.

"You Shall Be Filled"

Blessed is the hungers and thirsts for righteousness, for he shall be filled. Matthew 5:6

Hunger and thirst for God and His righteousness and you shall be filled. You want to trust Him? Be filled with His righteousness. You want to not doubt Him? Be filled with His presence. To trust God regardless of the situation, requires us to be filled with His

-126-

presence. Anything short of this will leave us doubting, worrying, frustrated, fearful and confused. You must follow the recipe to get the results. You must follow the instructions in the Word of God to get to a point of complete trust in God. Stop relying on material things to feel blessed; but look to God for joy, hope and peace based upon your intimate relationship with Him. Hunger and thirst for Him, until you know that you can rest in, trust in, and rely upon God regardless of the situation. If you will hunger and thirst for His righteousness, you shall be filled.

✳

Printed in the United States
By Bookmasters